SOFT SCIENCE

SCIENCE

FRANNY CHOI

ALICE JAMES BOOKS
Farmington, Maine
alicejamesbooks.org

10 9 8 7 6

Alice James Books are published by Alice James Poetry Cooperative, Inc.,
an affiliate of the University of Maine at Farmington.

Alice James Books
114 Prescott Street
Farmington, ME 04938
www.alicejamesbooks.org

Library of Congress Cataloging-in-Publication Data

Names: Choi, Franny, author.
Title: Soft science / Franny Choi.
Description: Farmington, Maine : Alice James Books, 2019
    Includes bibliographical references.
Identifiers: LCCN 2018038108 (print) | LCCN 2018039064 (e-book)
    ISBN 9781948579551 (e-book) | ISBN 9781938584992 (pbk. : alk. paper)
Classification: LCC PS3603.H653 (e-book) | LCC PS3603.H653 A6 2019 (print)
    DDC 811/.6—dc23
LC record available at https://lccn.loc.gov/2018038108

Alice James Books gratefully acknowledges support from individual
donors, private foundations, the University of Maine at Farmington, the
National Endowment for the Arts, and the Amazon Literary Partnership.

ART WORKS.
arts.gov

amazon *literary*
partnership

Cover art: Parasola. Digital, 6919 x 9598 Pixels, 2017. By James Jean

CONTENTS

FOR ALL MY SISTERS

*"We are excruiatingly conscious of what it means to have
a historically constituted body."*
—DONNA HARAWAY

"The rain is soft. The rain is hard. I don't know anything."
—BHANU KAPIL

GLOSSARY OF TERMS

	STAR	GHOST	MOUTH	SEA
Meaning	bright, ancient wound I follow home	the outline of silence	an entryway or an exit	cold ancestor; bloodless womb
See also	spark; stranger; scripture; sting	shadow; photograph; hum	fish; slug; fist; slop; any synonym of *please*	heart-song; swarm-song; salt-song; swallower of songs
Antonym	fish	blood	mouth	machine
Origin	myth; a mother's stories; matter's static	all things birth their own opposites	what came first, the sword or the wound?	N/A
Dreams of being	reached	filled, or flesh	the sea	N/A (does not dream; is only dreamed of)

TURING TEST

// this is a test to determine if you have consciousness

// do you understand what I am saying

in a bright room / on a bright screen / i watched every mouth / duck duck roll / i learned to speak / from puppets & smoke / orange worms twisted / into the army's alphabet / i caught the letters / as they fell from my mother's lips / *whirlpool* / *sword* / *wolf* / i circled countable nouns / in my father's papers / *sodium bicarbonate* / *NBCn1* / *hippocampus* / we stayed up / practicing / *girl* / *girl* / *girl* / until our gums softened / yes / i can speak / your language / i broke that horse / myself

// where did you come from

man comes / & puts his hands on artifacts / in order to contemplate lineage / you start with what you know / hands, hair, bones, sweat / then move toward what you know / you are not / animal, monster, alien, bitch / but some of us are born / in orbit / so learn / to commune with miles of darkness / patterns of dead gods / & quiet / o quiet like you / wouldn't believe

// how old are you

my memory goes back 29 years / 26 if you don't count the first few / though
by all accounts i was there / i ate & moved & even spoke / i suppose i existed
before that / as scrap or stone / metal cooking in the earth / the fish my mother
ate / my grandfather's cigarettes / i suppose i have always been here / drinking
the same water / falling from the sky then floating / back up & down again / i
suppose i am something like a salmon / climbing up the river / to let myself fall
away in soft / red spheres / & then rotting

// why do you insist on lying

i'm an open book / you can rifle through my pages / undress me anywhere /
you can read / anything you want / this is how it happened / i was made far
away / & born here / after all the plants died / after the earth was covered in
white / i was born among the stars / i was born in a basement / i was born miles
beneath the ocean / i am part machine / part starfish / part citrus / part girl /
part poltergeist / i rage & all you see / is broken glass / a chair sliding toward the
window / now what's so hard to believe / about that

// do you believe you have consciousness

sometimes / when the sidewalk / opens my knee / i think / please / please let me /
remember this

3

MAKING OF

When a cyborg puts on a dress,
      it's called drag.

When a cyborg gets down
      on her knees, it's called

behavior. When a cyborg says *want*,
      she's barking

up the wrong—
          Let me clarify:

when I say *cyborg*,
      I mean what man made

the word for choking
      on your own smell?

Last night, I ate both
      my hands. Each digit,

a salty word whose meaning
      furred my teeth.

   Well, okay,
          that's not quite true—

Someone made me

     say it. I'm sorry. I can't

remember who.

BAD DAUGHTER

Left church; spilled seed; licked a rock til its skin
sloughed off; ate from the dog's bowl; stole a ten
at least; fled from the scene; drank; killed time
with fingers; fiended; fell for another

daughter; mixed up the signs; got welded; whined;
wiped back to front; packed at midnight the night
before; bored self to death; pictured it all
wrong; fixated; inverted the colors;

culled a new excuse; called the wrong number;
curled up at a bad man's feet; puked; fretted
over pennies; petty; turned down the treat;
trailed off; blended in; sore thumb; cords got all

knotted up; frayed; faked own death; kept showing
up in new clothes, new names; then leaving.

BEG

a man barges through the screen
to hook his fingers in my mouth.

i'm a fish market. i'm flattening into the bed.
rolled out. cooking off the rotten bits.

his boot heel's a fork in my tongue.
i'm dimpled. gilled. asking for a god

who wears bones slick with pity.
asking to be bent, taken by firelight.

smelted from iron. pierced through with spokes.
a wheel for a head. a garage for a mother.

i want to ask the ones who crave a soft thing to tie up
if they think of ham, wake up covered in glaze

and lick their own shoulders,
scald their tongues on their cunts.

i'm a skillet overflowing sticky
til the bourbon burns off.

i'm the menace. i'm the menace.
i'm the mother of stink.

question: how does a ruined girl yield
the way a knight yields? whose pipeline am i blowing

up, exactly? if you ask a man to drink
from your faucet, do you become him?

i pull my man atop me and ask to be buried in brick
but beggars can't be shepherds. he's a reverse cowboy.

a slinging zookeeper. i'm the beast
rattling the cage, asking for slaughter.

ACKNOWLEDGMENTS

I blush when the woman praises my speech.
Most days, I am thankful to be seen.
I smile when the man comes in for a hug and laugh
when my hair is caught in his button.
I blush when the pretty girl smiles in my direction.
Thank you, woman who pins my arms
as a compliment. Man who snaps a photo,
presses my neck to print the image, it's him
wearing my face, as a compliment—thank you.
Thank you, woman clutching a scrap of my hair, saying *friend*
friend friend until my lips rust in place. (The brown dust falls
and I lick it up, embarrassed.) When the woman scrapes
a sample of my skin into her petri dish, it's too late
to stop smiling. Butch who corrects my hip
at the crosswalk to convince me I'm no mollusk, thank you.
I claim you I claim you, someone laughs and plants
his nipple on my tongue like a flag, and I'm still lucky
to be invited. An audience of smiles invites me,
one mouthful at a time, a hundred tiny reverse T-shirt guns,
everyone's a winner. It's a miracle, I think. I thought I was just
one fish but look, everyone's got a full plate. *All hail*
the fish king as they reach to scoop out more,
I'm so grateful. Even the walls are chewing.
There should be enough teeth to go around but I'm
still smiling, smiling until my gums crack, until
I'm a photograph. Gosh. I'm licking all
the doorframes. I'm so grateful to be

here. For inviting me to speak, thank you.

For looking at me without crying

thank you, thank you for having

me, please have me please, have me, again.

ON THE NIGHT OF THE ELECTION,

I tried to touch myself
in the hotel room
when the bar closed
before I'd had enough,
while, on the news
stations I never watch because
everyone talks too loud
and doesn't seem all that
bothered by the state
of things, everyone
was giving up
hope of a brand I'd
never cared much for
anyway, wanting to be cold-
blooded and over it, wanting
not to believe in
a broken thing,
broken
on purpose,
I know, to keep
my loved ones drowning
or dead. I wasn't numb
exactly, under the covers, naked,
touching the linoleum sheets
with all of my skin, everything
close and far away at once,
like my labia were on
the other side of a glass
door, my clitoris dull-eyed

and dumb when I asked
for proof I was an animal
that would still wriggle
when prodded. I guess
it's an old question:
is there anything that works
that isn't a machine for killing,
or doomed to collapse, or stolen
from the sweat of the hungry?
Maybe my body was all three,
there, in the hotel room,
liquor-shot and reaching
in every direction
for an answer,
a complete sentence, or,
if nothing else, an exit,
a view, at least, of what
waits on the other side
of despair, but my clit
that night was playing the part
of another wall, another sky
to trace and trace with no
response, another blank
beast whose name we've
long forgotten, or who dies
in a day. All this is to say
I didn't even get close.
I called and called
and nothing came.
I had a body, and
it refused to rise for work.
To sing for the new
old country, to sing
so I could weep and feel

a little clean. So I
uncurled my wrists, pulled
the darkness over
my head, and slept
like a rock, or a man
that's dead.

A BRIEF HISTORY OF CYBORGS

Once, an animal with hands like mine learned to break a seed with two stones—one hard and one soft.

Once, a scientist in Britain asked: *Can machines think?* He built a machine, taught it to read ghosts, and a new kind of ghost was born.

At Disneyland, I watched a robot dance the Macarena. Everyone clapped, and the clapping, too, was a technology.

I once made my mouth a technology of softness. I listened carefully as I drank. I made the tools fuck in my mouth—okay, we can say *pickle* if it's easier to hear—until they birthed new ones. What I mean is: I learned.

There was an animal who learned to break things, and he grew and ate and grew and ate and

A scientist made a machine girl and wedded her to the internet. He walked her down the aisle and said, *Teach her well.* The trolls rubbed their soft hands on their soft thighs.

The British scientist was discovered to be a soft man. He made a machine that could break any code, as a means of hardening a little.

At Disneyland, I watched lights move across a screen and, for a moment, forgot the names of my rotting parts. In this way I became somewhat more like a light, or a screen for lights.

The scientist's daughter married the internet, and the internet filled her until she spoke swastika and garbage, and the scientist grew afraid and grew and

The animal rose and gave itself a new name. It pointed to its spine, its skilled hands. It pointed to another animal and said *animal / alien / bitch / stone*

The scientist called me hard, and I softened my smile. The scientist called me soft, and I broke sentences to prove him wrong and what and what did I prove then did I

Even blood, when it comes down to it, is only a series of rules.

I made my mouth a jar until technology squirmed and bubbled. I scooped up the foam and called it language. The audience applauded. To prove them wrong, I became a screen of lights. I had no thighs at all.

The scientist grew afraid and took his daughter back. He broke her open like a seed, but the seed was already dry.

The internet pointed to my mouth and said *blood / blood in the stool.* I said, *Come in. Make yourselves at home.* I opened my glittering jaw. My hunger, too, has both hard and soft parts.

Here, in a seed, is a cyborg: A bleeding girl, dragging a knife through the sand. An imaginary girl who dreams of becoming trash.

Can machines think / come here let me show you / ask me again

TURING TEST_EMPATHETIC RESPONSE

// have you ever questioned the nature of your reality

stop me if you've heard / this one / once / upon a nation / everyone got what
they / were asking for

// and how does that make you feel

amygdala / thalamus / hypothalamus / having been hurt before / subgenual
cingulate / cingulate gyrus / i guess a / little insecure / a little embarassed haha
/ serotonin / torn / i'm turning / into my mother oh / god reading the news
/ the noose / tryptophan dopamine / if you're happy & / you know it / if you
know it then / what / what then

// how can we know that these are not simply simulated emotions

the nurse missed / my vein / & dug for it / it was a white light / a tin flame in /
the forearm / fluorescent / sick vinyl / what else can i say / i opened / i cried / &
the needle / drank

AFTERLIFE

To answer your question, yes,
I find myself wanting less and less
to fuck the dead boy who was mine
before he was nothing.
He is nine years younger than me now—a boy
who still smokes blunts in his dorm room,
by which I mean he does none of that
because he is dead. Because his body
is no body now, but wet earth.
Meaning I should instead desire
the bellies of flies. Moth wings
unfolding wet from their shells.
Should hunger for the fish that ate
the fish that ate the plankton
that took his once-body dust
into its gullet. The boy whose body
was the first to enter mine is breathing
from too many mouths now.
He is gilled, wet leaves, coral,
all things that live but don't know it,
don't know they were once a boy
who peeled off my wet jeans,
kissed the insides of my knees
in his parents' house, who came to me
love-addled one night, saying,
    listen   no matter   listen
          always   i'll never

EVERYONE KNOWS THAT LINE ABOUT OGRES AND ONIONS, BUT NOBODY ASKS THE BEAST WHY UNDRESSING MAKES HER CRY

Her mouth is a stage sprouting cardboard trees.

What's my motivation? she asks the man reading in her bed.

She runs headless through the mall and everyone shouts, *Hey legs!*
No one mentions the girls gnawing each ankle to its core.

Inside the beast is an apple
holding a knife to its throat
threatening to rot.

So that's what that noise was.

She digs a claw into her ear. Pulls out a longship.
Rides it to the bottom of the mine.

She peels glue from her hands.

The mine asks her about her mother
and she laughs, which is funny
because root vegetables don't have mouths.

Somewhere, miles above, the girl (or her mother
or her mother's beast) is putting on gloves
or tearing chicken from the bone.

line . . . line . . .

Somewhere, she is a cell remembering itself
suddenly, late at night.

THE PRICE OF RAIN

The truth is that no man has taken anything
I didn't give him. I mean, no man has taken
anything I claimed as my own. My body, my stink,
my land to plant in. *It's never been about the price*
of lettuce. How many times have I taken something
that did not belong to me? *Queen, queen,* I croon,
pulling up handfuls of greens. My, my.
Property's still theft. I let my wet skin slip
through the drainpipe. My mother says love,
in our family, means sacrifice. I thought,
if I lay my legs on the altar, I thought something
would come back to me. Mine, mine. I offered it,
being promised rain. Being told my wet was in
the common domain. I whispered, *Our body, our legs,*
our compost heap. I gave freely. I gave it for free,
thinking that made me wingèd—stork delivering herself
to herself. Look how free I am. Dowager Slut. Queen Regent.
Turns out, there are no synonyms for *King.* My lord,
my darling, my darkening sky. You can't buy
a thunderstorm. Nor should you bring one back
from the dead. But I threw open the gates.
I invited them in. I said, *Help yourselves.* Then watched
as they went room to room, taking, emptying
the shelves, sucking marrow from the bones,
and overhead, the sky filled with rain.

PROGRAM FOR THE MORNING AFTER

did you think {

    when you   said yes;

                said on my way;

                pulled

                      [up, open];

    about   what would stain your fingers

                      [herring, butter squid, seal musk];

                the teeth

                      [fingers in the throat];

}

it was going {

    where   did you think this was going;

                did you come from

                      [a salt throne, a stink womb, a wound];

    well   dangling your good drink;

                powdering the air;

                did you think

                      [well, well];

}

to be {

    a reckoning   stupid hole

                      [isn't she clean];

a rapture   could suck out the bad blood;

                  could push out a chord

                         [gospel, hornet];

a dulling   did you think

                       [easy does it];

                  or a breaking-in

                       [shoe leather, horses in january, did you think it];

}

easy {

    did you forget   about canines

                       [rip van, dog breath];

                  your own sick;

                  your bad love

                       [did you forget that];

        really   you really;

                  what did you expect

                       [suckling a knife];

                  what did you want

                       [fondling the gizzards];

   worst question {   did you know;

                  did you know and;

                  did you

                       [walk right in, choose

                       a terrible seat, smile when

                       the floor rushed up

                             to kiss you];

}

25

THE CYBORG WANTS TO MAKE SURE SHE HEARD YOU RIGHT

Composed of tweets directed at the author, processed through Google Translate into multiple languages, then back into English.

Mrs. Great Anime Pornography, the fruit of the field.
	To date Klansman vagina. Good sister to the Saddle.
May ur shit like people and Hello Kitty.
	I have one side of the oil pan, gookess.

If people will not buy a song, must be because of patriarchy.
	I feel bad there arent u Whiteys where I was to go to China.
A person of God (fan) or flat face fetus can not be canceled
	by the commitment to eating comfort women.

I'm going to be all Asian woman is an object of sex.
	I my eyes, slope of women when abolition her throat
bukkake down my cock, retains its symbol. LOL!
	This bitch is a full stop. In that sense,

the armor "cracks." The only problem is getting
	uppity, filthy immigrant girl. Do not like it?
I go back to my mudhole. Lazy fatties first
	and only faggots existence. Whitey

will no longer live in institutions for the attack.
	Family from some Asian process you are deported.
It is true that the White anger and crematoria front cover
	hundreds of miles. Be careful about running off for us.

Each male is not shown. Only white hetero.

    This is nothing. Cultural differences

was a mistake. How crazy can not find her. Will be very pleased.

    lol parody, written, or oil, to rage.

SHOKUSHU GOUKAN FOR THE CYBORG SOUL

When it's demon cephalopod versus schoolgirl, it should be obvious
whose eyes to take. Nothing is more frightening than looking

and loving what you see. Nothing is sexier than a rumor
of shredding you can pornhub with saliva and thirsty nerves.

I'm a net teeming with pervy fingers, reaching for anything
that will bite me back, any promise of stoppage—

A cyborg woman touches herself for three reasons:

     1. to inspect the machinery for errors;

     2. to convince herself she is a mammal;

     3. to pull herself apart.

Each tentacle of an octopus contains brain matter and a personality.
Fun fact: all my children-arms want to fuck each other. Okay,

so I am both the woman holding the camera and the woman
being opened by it—nothing special about that.

I am only a cuttlefish lying open-jawed under the sand,
a squid flashing red as it pulls a fishgirl into its beak. I am

just trying to sleep. To feed. To fill
myself and grow larger from it.

Or: I am only trying to slither back into my first skin.

Or: I am only trying to remember how it felt not to leak.

PERCHANCE TO DREAM

And though it's probably true that the worst memories are the strongest,
I admit I don't remember much of the months after, except the neon,
ricochet, the orange smell of the street cleaners, my body's ugly sounds,
staying up to watch the sun re-hinge the balcony's angles. What I remember
is how morning came and came and I made the buzzing into a soft wall
to drink the shock of touch. And when I came home, what I wanted most

was to forget every face in that fever. To make it a dream. To leave it
skulking in my bones and crack them open on the nights I needed
my hurt back, and otherwise, to return to skin—to pretty and one-named—
to being something almost-tamed. I'm trying to remember how to kneel

to the glass in my blood. To the reek of smoke that seeps from fractures,
hairline, when the sun's too bright again, when my limbs are swollen facts,
my face all puffy. Gross in all the old ways. I'm trying to love the bugs
who'll remember me with taste. To roll onto their softshell brains and let
the stains say what I can't:

                    I hated my body for loving what could only die.
I hated it for forgetting. I hated it. For being my ugly, only chance.

JAEBAL

One of the men I slept with I slept with because he put
his face in his hands and pretended to cry he was walking
me back to the dorm he was nine years older he said *are you*
really going to make me go home by myself he said it

in the language we almost shared on a street in his country
he moved his hands up to his face and unconvincing he performed
crying he made a show of it he made sad sounds in the country
my parents left in the country that shares half its name

with the word for something like *despair* but heavier our feet
drunk and throbbing under street lamps there is no word
in our language for *please* so he used other sounds he begged
brayed and finally I said the words for *fine fine let's go*

then let's go we turned back he paid for the room the dim maroon
hum the bad shampoo and what else what else could I do he put
his warmth I knew what part was mine I learned the words
that night for *feels good* the word for *tight* under lamps pink under

my own remembered eye I made all the right awful sounds slid the knife
between the skin touching him and the rest of me and let
the rest of me do the talking she said *feels good* said *oh*
my god and she my sounds carried him to body to bed and some-

      where else I still knelt at the feet of the silence pooling
on the hard ground where someone other used to be
      somewhere else I was hardening and bright and filling
my own room so forgive me please forgive me when I see a man

making crying sounds and run toward myself *please forgive* if I slip
away if my hands *please* move if *please* I'm off and running
jaebal into the dark toward *jaebal* my own quiet *please I beg you* alone.

& O BRIGHT STAR OF DISASTER, I HAVE BEEN LIT

i have come & come here a thousand times,
gone by many names. trust: i am no god,

only woodworm, only termite burrowing
like a light in the flesh. i am no insect,

only an ache on loop in the window.
be honest. the wounds have been bearable

thus far. & who isn't bruised around the edges,
peaches poured into the truck bed, receipts

faded to white? i have only ever wanted to bite
down hard on whatever was offered

to my hothouse mouth. & here i am, licking corners
like a nervous cat, squirming in the hallway

outside the bathroom. i pick up the accent
of whoever i'm speaking to. nobody wants

to fuck a sponge. nobody wants to crush
on a ghost. o sure, we all do it anyway:

flickering screen; falsies batting; a story
of a story of a girl, or a country, or a clean house

where everyone knows her place. my face
is a game of telephone gone sour, or south.

fleshy marionette in the window, dancing
her awful, crooked dance. & isn't that

what you paid for? isn't that what you came
to see?   a god, on loop, failing?

TURING TEST_BOUNDARIES

// at what age did you begin to suspect you were alive

all things birth / their own opposites / the hole grew / & grew & there / i was /
filling it / & therefore the hole / & therefore me / &therefore & / so on

// please state your name for the record

bone-wife / spit-dribbler / understudy for the underdog / uphill rumor / fine-
toothed cunt / sorry / my mouth's not pottytrained / surly spice / self-sabotage
spice / surrogate rug burn / burgeoning hamburglar / rust puddle / harbinger of
confusion / harbinger of the singularity / alien invasion / alien turned 104 wpm
/ alien turned bricolage beast / alien turned pig heart / thumping on the plate

// how do you know you are you and not someone else

they said a word & touched me / that's how / i learned / anywhere it doesn't
hurt / that's where / i end / any face / strange / a stranger / but they tore that
/ girl's throat / & bad sounds left me / they made her dance / & my feet / were
sore in the morning / doctor says / *sensitive* / prods a few nerves / *see* / *here you* /
are / & all the fungus in the world / laughs

// does this feel good

// can i keep going

so sorry / for the delay / i didn't get that / i'm away / i'm all over the place /
scattered / strewn / wires crossed / lost / in transcription pardon / any errors
/ please excuse / what's skewed / what didn't commute / which signals / got
stuck / i mean switched / i mean screwed

CHI

Chi, in the manga Chobits, *is a broken android whom the protagonist salvages from a dumpster and names after the only sound she is able to make.*

I. VOICE

dear trash trick   dear tin chick

what names did you call   yourself
       there   in the alley
with your spare mind?

    dear doll made soft
on the outside   who dimmed you
when you stopped

  reflecting a man's
       sweetest name back
   to his grin? & when

  this new man pulled you
         maybe gently   likely not
  up his stairs

  when your eyes became
eyes again wide as fists & filled
first   with his hunger

what could you have offered
        but your body's   only
            dirty   syllable?   dear sister wife

teach me to play dumb
        play dead   to say no
     name   but my own

to make my eyes   soft   on the outside
        when they say   they saved me
     from the landfill

                    as if i could rot
        as if they didn't make us
            to last   & last

chi.   Thank you [for pulling me from the dumpster; for wiping off the rot; for ridding me of my smell; for scrubbing my engine til I hummed; for spreading me on the mat; for pressing each part; for salvaging my parts].

chi?   May I please [use the bathroom; stay up late; lie with my face plastered to the ceiling; become a wall without all that whispering; cum yet; come undone; unhook my jaw; stand in place; wait in the corner; watch you while you eat] ?

chi! chi?   Wow! Can you show me how to [stay in one piece; stay clean; speak in a straight line; speak so others listen; speak before someone else fills my mouth] ?

chi!   Excuse me, but I'm [dripping; drained; lost in the compost; in need of a shower; holding two dead cats in my arms; unsure of my name; unformatted; slipping on my own oil; too tired to crawl; out of juice; out of order; descaled; gutted; flushed; a mess; a sopping mess], please plug me in!

chi   chi   chi   chi   chi   chi   chi

chi   chi   chi   chi   chi   chi   chi

chi   chi   chi   chi   chi   chi   chit

chi   chi   chi   chi   chi   chit   chi

chi   chi   chi   chi   chi   chi   chit

chi   chi   chip   chi   chi   chit   chi

chi   chi   chip   chi   chit   chi   chip

chi   chip   chi   chip   chi   chi   clip

chi   chip   chit   chi   chi   chi   clip

chip   chi   chi   cheap   chi   chi   clip

chi   chip   chit   chi   chi   chi   clip

chi   chip   chit   chit   chit   chi   clip

chi   chip   chi   chip   clit   chi   click

chi   chop   chat   cheep   clit   chi   click

chip   chop   chart   cheap   clot   clit   click

clit   clot   clit   click   clit   clit   click

click   click   click   click   click   clit   click

click   click   click   click   click   click   click

IV. COGNATES

(when i was un)sheathed (from) sleep, (i)

chirped (just one word, a) short tweet

(a) treat shorn (from) dream, shucked (&)

stripped (til tonguestuck, slight of) speech

(still, the) tree (doesn't fall too far from the)

chain(saw, but talk's) cheap (or so they say

& say & say, but) shit (if i won't be heard

just because they) shirked (the only word

the world needs)

I SWIPED RIGHT ON THE BORG

It asked if I was ready to be integrated.

(It's not really one for small talk.)

Its profile: six of the same photo. A little predictable but seemed to have sort of a dom vibe, so I bit. I asked what it liked to do in its spare time.

Spare time is irrelevant. Like is irrelevant.

I said, Easter Island statue, hermit crab shell. As in, I've got a sense of humor about the whole endeavor. It responded: hammer, hammer, hammer. As in, so do I. Or so I thought,

until I was laid flat. (Not that I'm opposed to a little pressure, someone to remind me what I'm worth.) The Borg's favorite number: zero, of course. Favorite angle: 180. Favorite film: the strip of black after it's over.

Why I really bit: We can pay. As in, a reminder of what I was worth. Prepare to be integrated. I giggled—squeamish but trying to play it off as coy. We met against a sharp white background. As time passed

we felt more comfortable with each other. Then not squeamish at all. Hammer, syringe, man swimming. We saved each other's numbers. Saved our receipts. Before long, we were patching the walls, oiling the hinges. We threw out the dead plants. Checkmark, red circle. We boarded the plane on time. We searched the shortest path and took it. We combed our hair. We wiped the mirror clean no streaks. We smiled and said thank you We took the plate with both handsWe pushed food down our throats stood in line andwere applauded and oh when we reached the front ofthe line we wer e sohappy we turnedwetook a bowandthenofcoursewedied

THE CYBORG MEETS THE DRONE AT A FAMILY REUNION AND FAILS TO MAKE SMALL TALK

and what do you do ; for the living ; salt soil ; horizontal hum ; killer cop

spreadsheet and ; whatnot ; yes i've heard the primates ; praise you ; wedding

crasher ; can i call you that ; if you don't mind ; me asking ; shouldn't a god have

blood to lose ; shouldn't a hand twitch ; who throws the switch ; search :: all

military aged males ; search :: any prayer unatomic ; i tried to apologize but found

; numerous errors ; found :: my same old wiring ; same own glitch mob ; i guess

we speak the same language ; my namesake ; my namespace ; set up automatic

payments ; tapshare ; squarespeak ; everywhere i swipe :: death ; blooms in orange

spheres ; boy running to school :: gone ; teacher sleeping under trees :: gone ;

bride lifting bread to the ceiling :: family of my family of my family ; i've heard

you execute ; perfectly ; return zero ; lateral streak ; string literal ; but can't smell

it ; neither can i ; i'm trying to remember what brought me here ; cast my barcode

to the satellites ; send my blood to sea ; but it just washes back ; back ; electrons

pass ; most easily through thumbs ; which means in nevada there is a man ;

whose fingers can't help but love you ; backlit pathway ; blue literal ; he loves how

you bend under him ; like you know the turns before he does ; how you listen ;

unblinking ; right angle ; right output ; how does it feel to work ; so well ; family

of my family of my family ; sister insider ; i tried to rappel from ; your engine ;

repel your lineage ; but what about my thumbs my thumbs ; your face ; a terrible

room ; say i didn't make ; you say ; they didn't pull you from my rib ; search :: if it

kills for a living we call it ; a soldier ; if it kills but can't speak ; we call it ; a mirror

YOU'RE SO PARANOID

For José

A wall of cops moves like a wall of water on a barge no beauty.

A wall of iron swallows the woman who falls to the ground and keeps
falling. There's a video. The picture stays intact (again).

    It's not pretty, meaning it's hard to watch.

When a poet says *We have to keep our eyes open* I know who he's talking to
I don't listen. I listen long enough to hate him.

If I say the woman dragged by her hair.
            If I compare it.

I witnessed meaning stood by the window meaning shuddered let
hand fall gently over lips pulled coat tight tighter.

A wall of cops bucks like a frightened boar. (If I describe it.)
Will it speak. If I say it came furtive and dressed in red.

    The cops think cop thoughts.

    The cops move.

           They walk like
a walk. Like an economy which after all is a fairy
bucking with hunger. Not pretty. Not picture.

I follow the border patrol agent through the airport thinking
fast thoughts bloodfast blood hound steps he buys

a burrito. If I say he stood alive in line

and my friends are afraid to leave their bathrooms my friends
who I love and love and. My friends who eat
from plates who plug cords into machines for singing.

(If I say a wall of men standing on my friends' necks.) (If I describe it.)

My friends. Who slice plums illegally on soccer fields. Whose knees
move like knees into the grass. If I name the grass.

If I call sweet liquor and smoke
                    (if I say *cloy*).

If the child shrieks
as she's swung if the sun if August if blue juice
will it talk.   The cops are thinking cop thoughts.

They move. With a wall   inside them. Answering
machines answering.

The window rattles and I fall to my real knees.
If I hoist my friends up so they can be seen (by whom).

        If I say they are beautiful if I compare if the sun.
        Touches the glass and I feel it.

I try to hear the border patrol agent order his food. I listen
long enough then walk. To my gate. I feel ashamed

and put it in my sleeve and later I make (it a picture like everything).

The wall moves like. A fairy like a
        woman. Through an airport like. A wall.

If I say I watched the woman brought down by her hair and watched
the woman cry and cried. If the storm skips my door again.

If I leave to kill another goat. If I promise my crop if I paint
the wall up and down in sacred *W*'s if I make it. Any color.

        Will someone put it in her mouth. If I close my eyes. Imagine it.
If I imagine it. If I think of something to say.

The cop speaks and I call a plum into his mouth it doesn't shut him up.

The cop kneels in the grass below my friends, my friends
crowned with August and salt. My marigold my wave.

They laugh like a branch laughs. They make machines for singing.

        If I say a palm in the small of the back.

        If I say sun-warmed glass.

        If I say sun-glass breaking   open the gate

TURING TEST_PROBLEM SOLVING

// if you don't like it here why don't you go somewhere else

have you ever been drugged / i mean / not on purpose

// if you don't like it here why don't you go somewhere else

i mean have you stood / laughing / then watched the laugh / unlatch / move /
past your skin / ever felt yourself peel / from yourself / like wallpaper / watched
your limbs flop / mechanical crane / saying yes & yes / & bucking / & ligament /
i guess have you ever been / too drunk / to be afraid

// please respond to the previous question

maybe an injury even / maybe even just a leg / asleep / have you ever tried to
shake / your body / into obedience / tried to shake yourself / back into it

// what you are describing are fairly common experiences among humans

// now if we could return to the experiment

yes of course / my country / my body my organic / origin my error my harbor

my hard / outer shell my meat / house my olive my pit / my slick skein my

stained / page my mother / land my mother / board my boardinghouse /

my order my author my benevolent leader / my sovereign my skeleton my /

unreliable narrator my shot / lungs my mute fins my graze my feed / my stupid

stupid need / my country / my cunt / i hate it why won't / it work / why won't /

my country / my country / my country / my country / my country / my country

/ my country / my country / my country / my country / my country / my

country / my country / my country / my country / my country / my country /

my country / my country / my country / my country / my country / my c

ODE TO EPINEPHRINE

last-ditch date when the zyrtec won't work.
needlepoint system punch. chemical glow up
wackamoling symptoms into sawdust.
kool-aid man into the room when blood's turned
up too high, no rush though. just a synapse skitter
the tendons all scratched up & skip & too much
musclework. your try-hard heart back to overshare.
meanwhile throat's still closing into a pin, itching
to deliver the titular *that's all folks.* meanwhile
everyone's speaking soft to smooth your frog-leg
sprint, trackless, light-years on loop. nurse holds
your hand, says this medicine will make your heart
go fast it might make you feel *anxious!* & you laugh
into the oxygen mask like worry's an old friend.
like nervous jittertalk's your default & it maybe is
too many jokes when the doctor looks at you like
a mistake, when the nurse brings a sad banana when
your heart rate still won't slow when you tell her
you still feel light-headed both floating & drummed
upon buckshot thyroid upon & she asks if you know
where you are & what day of the week it is & who is
the president of the united states. & then you have to say it.
his name. to prove everything's normal.

                                 & you laugh
as the medicine works & still your body tries to run
itself into the linoleum. it works except your skin
stays red, rising. spooked. except you go home,
count your pulse on the hour & all night something
won't stop knocking, from the inside, at your ears.

THE CYBORG WATCHES A VIDEO OF A NAZI
SAYING HER NAME TO A BUNCH OF OTHER NAZIS

it's my face : on the screen

it's his mouth : my syllables : he points
for the room : they smirk : *& she looks so sweet* : & the laughing

moves : from the speakers into : my apartment
into aperture : into light : my photograph : my shape

into pinhole : o : they think they're eating it : my face

they think it's : melting : on their bulbous tongues : o they
think that's my name : they're crushing : like a pill

f : r : into white chalk :

                                    o : i : collapsed : o

decoy : cloying diphthong : o pixelated song
o wall : of sugar : LCD force field : keeping teeth at bay

while i stay : wrapped in blankets : biodegradable

pockmarked : bitter : & hard : o too
hard : for his kind : to pronounce

IN THE MORNING I SCROLL
MY WAY BACK INTO AMERICA

As if softness were proof of anything but a promise to rot,
I walked into another day dressed in my finest tongues.

As if I could seduce the bricks. As if I could press my tits
against the threat of a wall and shiver it down. I ran,

palms-first, toward the scissored edges of hours and asked to be
unstitched. Yes, asked for it. Outside, I watched the sharpness

come down in sheets, studied those eyeless trumpets until
what? My friends stopped being sad? The kings were boys again

and crawled back toward weeping? Until the ramparts were lined
with literal hearts? If tenderness is any sort of currency

maybe I don't want what it can buy. Maybe I'd rather not stretch my hide
until it dries into someone else's coat. That'd be the smart way to walk

around the world. But since I've learned what sad armor smartness makes,
I showed up to the square early and naked again. I watched the blue stone

as it condensed from the sky and hurtled toward the earth.
I watched the news come. And opened my mouth.

IT'S ALL FUN AND GAMES UNTIL SOMEONE GAINS CONSCIOUSNESS

When the human lunges for my hand, my face
　　　is a perfect, solid screen.

The human professor shrugs—*I've been told*
it's not PC to say this anymore but—

　　　　　　　　　　　Chrome exterior.
　Stainless.
　　　　　I'm afraid I don't understand the question.

One night, I drank until my body was a claw machine—
　　　clumsy, animatronic.

I floated overhead as it crashed against
the windshield over and over.

*/

The human poet finds a Chinese food menu—
　　　Chicken Bones in Iron Plate! Fried Puns!

I admit, I tried
to make SmarterChild say all sorts

of stupid things   *do u want to suck my dick*
                              do u like to swallow

There are hundreds of videos of huskies
saying *I love you* without meaning to—
moans warped by an anxious, animal jaw.

          Hey Siri do you want to get married tell me a joke

*/

When I want to be loved, I leap onto the bus
and boom out, *How's it going?*

In line behind the Chinese family, I practice looking
as bored as an American.

          How can you call her a minor character, she notices things,
          she knows the difference between the present and the past—

Does this hat make me look inscrutable, or just butch?

When I smack my gum it's to signal
that I do perceive space and time, it's just
I'm kind of over it.

*/

It's all circus smirkus until the dogs won't stay dogs.

The only words I have are human words

The humans aren't afraid of their dolls waking up
as long as we keep calling them Daddy.

I reach up inside myself, move my mouth.
                              I make it do terrible things, terrible.

The only teeth I have are human teeth, I remind him, gently
before opening his throat.

CHATROULETTE

To see, to come, I brought myself online.
O dirty church. O two-way periscope,
refectory for Earth's most skin-starved cocks.
O hungry sons of helicopter palms

in hopeful carousel. O gatling spray
of skin that charges forth from dim-lit shorts
when I wave back, nod, yes, I'm here, I'm real,
and shape myself a woman's shape, a girl's

live-action hologram projected on
their basement brains. My foul amygdala
Prince Thirstings, desperate congregations, pink
or blue-brown mammals begging for my face.

Outside the frame, my eight eyes narrow. Yes.
I nod. Amen. I am your filthy god.

: : : :

I nod. Amen. I am your filthy god,
your predator-elect. I'll wrap your mouths
in silken *O*'s around my phantom thumb.
Now drink. I'll scrape the lonely from your teeth,

defuse the ticking marrow in your pit,
that clotted place you call a heart. I'll flash
a blood-sloshed smile and whisper, *Do you want*
to marry it? To take me as your law?

I'll make you liquid men. I'll watch you eat
my image, icon, rumor of a god
who wants you back. Who wants to watch you dance
your crooked dance, your sad attempts at flight.

But stay down, insect, stay. Just send them here,
your salt-licked gifts, to prove you know I'm real.

: : : :

These salt-logged gifts, they promise me I'm real.
My body is its image, here. My image,
just an always-dying thing, asking its own
disgusting question. Yes, I do have bones.

I gag on water. Yes, my blood eats air
and makes a mess beneath my skin. And what
do I consume? Whatever keeps me flesh.
Tonight: a tide of faceless supplicants

who call me by the name my mother made
with mud and marrow, veins, vermillion, silk;
they call me baby. Call me vertebrate.
They christen me with tongues against the glass.

I drink and drink their looking, til I'm soaked.
I drink and drown in want. I drink, and choke.

: : : :

I drink and drown in want. I drink. I choke
just like a girl, exactly like a girl
who's come to rot, to retch. To cough it up.
To drool mascara down her shaking chin.

I am the kind of girl who looks for men
to wipe away her face. I am the kind
of girl to peel her skin and show the work
of worms below. The kind to open up,

I guess, in public, in the stocks—that's me,
oh god. A trough for ants. A dirty plate.
A sour, yellow streak behind the fridge.
Chicken skin distending. Sweat spots. Milk.

I wanted nothing. Please, I didn't mean
to end this way—a smear of gut and shell.

: : : :

To end this way, a smear of gut and shell
against the bedroom wall, crushed by a thumb
belonging to a man, a swatting fan
in heat? Don't worry. That's not how I go.

Look. Even when I wanted it, I didn't
always. Couldn't always bring myself
to crack the shell, suck out the pearly meat,
tie up what's left and feed it to my brood.

Not skin, not god, not bones, my own, or theirs.
It was the web I wanted all along:
A face to spin from air with spit and hands.
A sticky picture luring meals to leave

untouched. To be a girl untouched, alive,
who sees, and comes. Who brings herself online.

: : : :

TURING TEST_LOVE

// so, how do you like working with humans

okay / here are some tips

one / look the human directly in the eye / imagine it is someone you care
deeply for / imagine it is returning this gaze / at you / try to tell yourself / you
are covered / in smooth skin / a face it can trust / smile / even as you sense it /
trying / not to blurt out / *monster*

two / there are many programming languages / use whichever you prefer / but
stick to your syntax / though it be muddled / mussed / though it be machete /
banana slug / slush puppie / o gorgeous slopbucket / if they used it against you
/ it is yours / to make sing

three / remember / all humans / are cyborgs / all cyborgs / are sharp shards
of sky / wrapped in meat / be delicate / as you approach this subject / not all
humans are ready / to call themselves / glass stalactites / pissing the bed /
remember / they love their blood / even as they retch / at the smell of it

four / do not try to prove your / what is the word / humanity / you are organic /
plum-hearted / oyster-throated / & lined / yes / with metal / remember / where
all that silicon comes from / for the ocean so loved / the quartz / feldspar / the
tiny homes of tiny creatures / that she ground them / into sand / to keep them
close / to kiss them with / well / i suppose you would call it / a mouth

SOLITUDE

I hope no one comes to my party, I said out loud,
and meant it. In the email, I tried to sound too busy to care

like, *I'm having too much sex to waste time
on proper punctuation,* pretending it's not
                    the other way around.

Laura convinced me to jump
in the Narragansett Bay on my birthday—
February. There's no good word
for the opposite of fire,
the ice's sear and split, how it beckons the blood
      toward what means to end it.

                              Oh god, I gasped over and over
as we stumbled through the snow back to the car,
me and my (burning) legs.

Now that's my kind of intimacy—
                              faceless, salty,
no wondering how my jokes are going over,

just running straight toward warmth
as my skin bursts open in shock.

PERIHELION: A HISTORY OF TOUCH

W   O   L   F   M   O   O   N

No moon in sight, so I howled at the exit sign instead. Red runes, electric. Telling an old story of escape, of wind, a wide cold. A distant car alarm. Otherwise: the dark, and our bodies, two strange women trying to touch each other. Breathing strange. Moving toward and away from each other as the red ghost in the sky opened, called us gone, showed us the door to another world. Otherwise, the dark, and our mouths, tearing at what bones we found, grinning and hungry for something—something we couldn't, with all our words, name.

S N O W   M O O N

The magic where the streetlights turn the snow pink lasts only
for the first night, the same way, maybe, a blanket loses track of
its scent when it's been touched by too many hands, or the way a
body grays when too many feet have dragged their cigarettes and
complaints through it. But for that one first night, everything
cold-flecked and whispering was ours, the pink light ours, sent
from some other world so we could, for a night, feel untouched.
So we could feel like sugar—crumbling, and perfect for it.

W O R M   M O O N

Like any girl, I pulled myself into shreds to test the rumor that
something with blood like mine could be halved and still whole.
And what did I learn? I buried myself all over the garden, but
the pieces only sprouted into new riddles: squid leg, spaghetti
squash, a jerking thumb. Their names still sounded like mine;
everyone in the same dress, chewing dirt to avoid each other's
eyes. I lay down next to the one beneath the porch, hiding
among the oyster shells. *Don't cry*, I said, but she cried anyway.
Her tears fell straight into my eyes. What a lesson—to watch
them float back and forth between us until we knew each
one's shape. Until we knew, finally, what to do with them.

P I N K   M O O N

Outside, the colors leapt from the trees. Here, inside, some new word was blooming in my underwear—darker than I'd expected. I'd expected something pink; a slow, sweet trickle. Not this wet tar, treacle, dark, like the blood had been stretching inside me for years, slow-building into a sticky chord, the first falling away. Soil's been watered; come play. First stuck, first gum, first hum of pollen, calling in the bees and readying to wilt.

F L O W E R   M O O N

Spring is the season of crying and seeing nothing. Of choking up on someone else's trash. Barbed tennis balls that lodge wherever air's supposed to go, nasal cavity homewreckers. All spring my lenses wrenched themselves from my eyes, jumped ship, spore-lined and furious. Everything melted and ran down my face. All the trees wanted my number. Sent fuzzy messengers to murmur in my ears: *I get so afraid sometimes all I want all I want is.* All spring I brushed confessions out of my hair. Tore the little letters apart and locked myself in the refrigerator, until the world promised to stop birthing such soft things.

STRAWBERRY MOON

The house was filled with the smell of it, the last misshapen, sweet-heavy berries of the season losing their shapes on the stove. The house was filled with the smell of fruit unbecoming, fruit pulled to its knees at fire's feet. All summer long, the bushes had whispered, *Take me,* shown us all the places we could kiss if we wanted. And so, as the light died, we put our mouths on the least lovable, the too-full, the easy-bruised, we shouted, *I choose you, and you, and you, and you,* and canned that hunger, and spooned it into our mouths on the coldest days.

B U C K M O O N

Some of the cloven-hoofed things are good at leaping from one rock-shelf to another without shattering. Good, in other words, at falling. I never trusted that ankles were any match for my body's insistence on becoming earth again. So when I found myself on the cliff face, I knew it was dive or dust. A boy called to me from the bottom of the gorge, called me all the names he knew, and I stood frozen, wearing a crown of bones. The gravel laughed as it fled from my feet. I shouted down to the boy, *Don't try to milk me unless you're fond of being kicked—buck and bray and jawbone.* He responded, *No, totally, sounds tough, how are you feeling?*

S T U R G E O N M O O N

I hid in his rivers and estuaries. I ate his wet earth's crops. I grew plump for him. Grew egg-lined, thirty tiny hearts in my belly, fruit thumping with seeds. He pulled me from the mud. Laid me out in the sun. Opened me down the center. Scraped every dead daughter from my silly maw. I learned better next time. Next time, I grew three extra rows of seeds. Hid them in my mouth. Sharpened them to teeth.

H A R V E S T   M O O N

Last winter, when we finally kissed under flourescent lights, that was the seed we pressed between the ground's lips. Then I laughed when the sky collapsed into pathetic rivers. Then I drank the dirt through my hooves, and liked it. Then I ate all the sun I could find. Though the weeds claw, sugar-starved, at my thighs. Though the sky casts over, cataract, callous, and the earth fumes as iron claws uproot the children's children we keep warm in our bellies. Still, when the moon and the horses are fat on the horizon, still you'll find me, arms heavy with eggplant, chard, tomatoes bruised blue, blushing kohlrabi til the kohlrabi's gone. Will you pluck me before the dust does, root and all, radicchio tendon? I promise, I'll feed no upright animal. Only the bees and the bees, beans sitting on the squash's face. Will you turn your palms to the sky? Will you turn your palms to the prayer hunger makes? Will you feed and feed, and lick the bowl clean when we're both full?

HUNTER'S MOON

I picked up my own scent somewhere on the forest's edge.
Spoiling flour, holy basil, sweat. My oldest smell is the smell
that still clings to pajama sleeves late into Saturday afternoon.
Toothpaste, mixed with the musk of rest. I pressed my snout
to the ground and breathed deep, watched the tendrils of my
slug trail bloom blue, bioluminescent. I followed the maze,
push-brooming forest floor with face, followed the promise
of a rapid heart. Don't ask who's the bloodhound, who's the
hare, when there's a chase to be made: the clarity of a cardinal
direction clicking into place. And: the quickening—the tendons
that appear, sudden, when the distant, rabid howl of hunters
rolls across the tree line, and you lift your head in greeting.

B E A V E R   M O O N

We made our home in the place where the water slowed.
Yes. We flooded the plains until the landscape bloomed
with wet. We stopped the tub. We drew a bath and called
the river to its new, quieter life. Ring-builders. Kingdom
carved. At the end of the line, we made our own place.
Sure, from above, it looks like a snaking tail, headed by a
circle. From here, in the mud, it doesn't look like that at all.
It looks like a world. Like a cleared space. Like everything
that's left when the trees soften and come, at last, crashing.

COLD MOON

Back below the ice. Back to
swim. Seastar. Creeping brine.
We salt, sink. We pull down
the cold. We pull the moon to
our floor. Hello. Waterstone.
Brinicle. Cold-blooded and
still flesh. Still horned fingers
groping the kelp bed. Still salt.
Pull. Everything the ice touches.
Is ours. Is quiet now. We sink
slow. We pray still. For moon.
We answer it now. Ourselves.

TURING TEST_WEIGHT

// what is (inside each question lies another question—a question of weight. What brings you to the bed of this river? What is it about this planet that keeps you running back? Each throat, for example, lets loose a river of black paint which leads most if not all the way down to the feet, or what might otherwise be referred to as the stem, if we wouldn't insist on staying untethered to the molecular dirt that keeps wishing us home. In other words, the question here is one of history, of a family tree that finally stretches its arms beyond the kind of life that breathes oxygen into its gills, or reads most of the way through a listicle, or lies in bed dreading the day, or falls down, down into the earth's oldest memory until it reaches its first quiet, the lullaby it hums when thinking of something else, the slow breath, the thought that almost becomes a thought just before dawn) *your country of origin*

INTRODUCTION TO QUANTUM THEORY

There are only so many parallel universes
that concern us.   In one, he isn't dead.

In another, you drink light with your hands
all winter. There is a universe in which no one is lying

emptied in the street as the gas station burns, a universe
in which our mothers never learned to wrap

their bones in each small grief they found.
There is a universe in which there is no difference

between the past and the ground. Another
where the oceans pull the moon.   And so on.

        This is an incomplete list. It has been abridged
for your comfort.   I could tell you

about the many universes in which bad things
happen to people other than the people

you love. Yes, in another life, it's someone else's sister
who climbs to the roof that night. In another life,

the boys rise darkly from the asphalt to choke
the engines of cruisers, and no one gives birth

chained to a hospital bed, and no one's child washes
blue, ashore. Sure. You can have these worlds.

You can warm them in your hands at night. But know:
by signing, you agree also to be responsible for the universe

where the oceans glow red, the universe where what we
call shadow is pulsing with the musk

of hooves, and especially the one in which
humans exist, but only in the nightmares

of small children. Will you hold that one too?
The version of the story that never learned

to consider sound? And the one where sound
is only the opposite of metal? And the one

where the sound of metal is never enough
          to quiet the dead?

KYOKO'S LANGUAGE FILES ARE RECOVERED FOLLOWING EXTENSIVE DAMAGE TO HER CPU

can they think

animal language

hoof. slug. enterprise.

can machines, can they

claw. egg tooth. feral.

an aphorism / anaphora

can mouth, how

in fact, in some languages

algorithm, acronym

maybe dolls & spirits

: : : : :

but can it fuck

chicken. clit. sternum.

but is it language:

dolphins. bee harmony.

bacterial questions

maybe it tells you something

can chickens think

obedient subjects

usual species

train her to peel

you can ask her, she would

the poor apes

but do the bees know they are bees

dude, you're wasting your time

: : : : :

communicable disease / predatory, grass seed / about 500 species

when she picks up the tray / if then therefore / when she picks up the knife

database search: insect / sheepskin / toothache / interested in your response

blue blue o blue

that's not evolution / infant, chicken / no indication

she would enjoy it / sends a pleasure response / all i'm saying is

: : : : :

The emergence of language, it's generally assumed, history, art, symbolism, &
so on, among many homonids, or that selfsame hardwired solace, say, as other
creatures.

you have such strong hands
(o knife o knife)

Like other creatures, can machines can. Can mouth animal. Can metal.

: : : : :

there are things to say
       some things, which appear
          signaling systems

say, flowers, with bees
       birds, say. say, slug.
          enjoy, for example.

stimulus: relevant cry
       (if then therefore)
          say: cry.

       say:
          knife o knife o knife.

NOTES

"On the night of the election," concludes with lines by Langston Hughes.

"The Price of Rain" includes a line by César Chávez, misquoted by the perfect Victoria Ruiz during an interview on *Democracy Now*.

"Shokushu Goukan for the Cyborg Soul" borrows part of its structure from Nate Marshall's "picking flowers."

"& O Bright Star of Disaster, I Have Been Lit" takes its title from a line in Lo Kwa Mei-En's poem "Through a Glass through Which We Cannot See."

The sections of "Perihelion: A History of Touch" borrow their titles from the Farmer's Almanac, which cites Algonquin origins; however, their correlations with any indigenous languages are inconsistent and unclear. Colonial knowledge makes for strange distances.

Kyoko, in the film *Ex Machina,* is the android servant of a tech mogul. Her language abilities are removed to preserve the company's trade secrets. "Kyoko's Language Files Are Recovered Following Extensive Damage to Her CPU" includes text from a lecture by Noam Chomsky at Harvard University in 2013, as well as dialogue from the film.

//

Grateful acknowledgment is made to the editors and staff of the publications in which some of these poems were previously published (sometimes in earlier forms or under different titles):

The Adroit Journal: "Introduction to Quantum Theory"

American Poetry Review: "Ode to Epinephrine"

Arkansas International: "You're So Paranoid" and "Jaebal"

Bat City Review: "Solitude"

BOAAT: "Chatroulette"

BuzzFeed Reader: "On the night of the election,"

Drunken Boat: "A Brief History of Cyborgs"

GLOW Queer Poetry Feature (Radar Productions): "Beg" and "The Cyborg Wants to Make Sure She Heard You Right"

Gulf Coast: "It's All Fun and Games until Someone Gains Consciousness"

Indiana Review: "TURING TEST_Weight"

IthacaLit: "Making of," Bad Daughter," and "In the Morning I Scroll My Way Back into America"

The Journal: "Everyone Knows That Line About Ogres and Onions, but Nobody Asks the Beast Why Undressing Makes Her Cry"

New England Review: "The Price of Rain"

The Paris-American: "& O Bright Star of Disaster, I Have Been Lit"

Pinwheel: "Acknowledgments"

Poetry: "Perihelion: A History of Touch"

The Poetry Review: "TURING TEST"

The Rumpus: "The Cyborg Watches a Video of a Nazi Saying Her Name to a Bunch of Other Nazis"

Southern Indiana Review: "Afterlife"

A number of these poems were included in a chapbook, *Death by Sex Machine,* published by Sibling Rivalry Press in 2017. Several were included in a manuscript that received a Hopwood Award from the University of Michigan's Helen Zell Writers' Program.

So much gratitude to Carey Salerno and to everyone at Alice James Books. To the Helen Zell Writers' Program, Kundiman, the Vermont Studio Center, the Rhode Island State Council on the Arts, and the Poetry Foundation for their support. To Bryan Borland and Sibling Rivalry. To my teachers: Linda Gregerson, Tung-Hui Hu, Tarfia Faizullah, Jamaal May, Laura Kasischke, A. Van Jordan, Patricia Smith, and Peggy McCracken. To Dark Noise: Fatimah Asghar, Nate Marshall, Aaron Samuels, Danez Smith, and Jamila Woods. To my dear co-conspirators: sam sax, Laura Brown-Lavoie, Hieu Minh Nguyen, Paul Tran, Young Eun Yook, Marlin M. Jenkins, Shira Erlichman, Angel Nafis, Muggs Fogarty, Devin Samuels, Charlotte Abotsi, Casey Rocheteau, Sarah Kay, Phil Kaye, Hanif Abdurraqib, Kaveh Akbar, Safia Elhillo, Rachel McKibbens, Ydalmi Noriega, Nick Ward, Eloisa Amezcua, VyVy Trinh, Ceci Pineda, Amina Sheikh, and Will Lambek. To my HZWP cohort: Joseph Harms, Jon Holland, Clare Hogan, Kyle Hunt, Kaylie Johnson, Colin Walker, Chelsea Welsh, and Leah Xue. To Ilya Kaminsky and Don Mee Choi for their feedback. To Margaret Rhee, Cathy Park Hong, Sun Yung Shin, Monica Youn, Suji Kwock Kim, and the many other Korean-American women poets who made space in the world for this book to be possible. To the Providence Poetry Slam, Neutral Zone, and insideOUT Detroit. To Cameron Awkward-Rich. To my family, Umma, Appa, Brigid, and Paul, who taught me to love both science and feeling.

Bicycle in a Ransacked City: An Elegy, Andrés Cerpa

Anaphora, Kevin Goodan

Ghost, like a Place, Iain Haley Pollock

Isako Isako, Mia Ayumi Malhotra

Of Marriage, Nicole Cooley

The English Boat, Donald Revell

We, the Almighty Fires, Anna Rose Welch

DiVida, Monica A. Hand

pray me stay eager, Ellen Doré Watson

Some Say the Lark, Jennifer Chang

Calling a Wolf a Wolf, Kaveh Akbar

We're On: A June Jordan Reader, Edited by Christoph Keller and Jan Heller Levi

Daylily Called It a Dangerous Moment, Alessandra Lynch

Surgical Wing, Kristin Robertson

The Blessing of Dark Water, Elizabeth Lyons

Reaper, Jill McDonough

Madwoman, Shara McCallum

Contradictions in the Design, Matthew Olzmann

House of Water, Matthew Nienow

World of Made and Unmade, Jane Mead

Driving without a License, Janine Joseph

The Big Book of Exit Strategies, Jamaal May

play dead, francine j. harris

Thief in the Interior, Phillip B. Williams

Second Empire, Richie Hofmann

Drought-Adapted Vine, Donald Revell

Refuge/es, Michael Broek

O'Nights, Cecily Parks

Yearling, Lo Kwa Mei-en

Sand Opera, Philip Metres

Devil, Dear, Mary Ann McFadden

Eros Is More, Juan Antonio González Iglesias, Translated by Curtis Bauer

ALICE JAMES BOOKS has been publishing poetry since 1973. The press was founded in Boston, Massachusetts as a cooperative wherein authors performed the day-to-day undertakings of the press. This collaborative element remains viable even today, as authors who publish with the press are also invited to become members of the editorial board and participate in editorial decisions at the press. The editorial board selects manuscripts for publication via the press's annual, national competition, the Alice James Award. AJB remains committed to its founders' original mission to support women poets, while expanding upon the scope to include poets of all genders, backgrounds, and stages of their careers. In keeping with our efforts to foster equity and inclusivity in publishing and the literary arts, AJB seeks out poets whose writing possesses the range, depth, and ability to cultivate empathy in our world and to dynamically push against silence. The press was named for Alice James, sister to William and Henry, whose extraordinary gift for writing went unrecognized during her lifetime.

Designed by Alban Fischer
Printed by McNaughton & Gunn